QUANTUM LEAPS

10 Steps to Help You *Soar*

simple truths®
Your Destination For Inspiration
an imprint of Sourcebooks, Inc.

GLORIA MAYFIELD BANKS

Editing by: Alice Patenaude

Photo Credits
Cover: front, author photo by Ernest Washington Studios Inc., stylist: Dr. Keith Harley, Iakov Kalinin/Shutterstock, tomertu/Shutterstock; back, Nik Merkulov/Shutterstock
Internals: page 1, author photo by Ernest Washington Studios Inc., stylist: Dr. Keith Harley, Iakov Kalinin/Shutterstock, tomertu/Shutterstock; page 4, Preto Perola/Shutterstock; page 5, Nik Merkulov/Shutterstock; page 6, tomertu/Shutterstock; page 13, BlueLela/Shutterstock; page 19, Andrey Burmakin/Shutterstock; pages 20–21, Ingrid Maasik/Shutterstock; page 29, Olivier Le Moal/Shutterstock; pages 30–31, Dudarev Mikhail/Shutterstock; page 37, Ideas_supermarket/Shutterstock; pages 38–39, Ioan Panaite/Shutterstock; page 42, Jojje/Shutterstock; page 44, Sashkin/Shutterstock; page 48, Oleksiy Mark/Shutterstock; pages 50–51, arek_malang/Shutterstock; page 55, dreamerve/Shutterstock, Madlen/Shutterstock; pages 56–57, LilKar/Shutterstock; page 61, nasirkhan/Shutterstock; pages 62–63, Kevin Day/Shutterstock; pages 68–69, Jaochainoi/Shutterstock; pages 76–77, Warren Goldswain/Shutterstock; pages 82–83, Peshkova/Shutterstock; pages 84–85, wavebreakmedia/Shutterstock; page 89, Ideas_supermarket/Shutterstock; page 92, author photo by Ernest Washington Studios Inc, stylist: Dr. Keith Harley, Hasloo Group Production Studio/Shutterstock.

Published by Simple Truths, an imprint of Sourcebooks, Inc.
P.O. Box 4410, Naperville, Illinois 60567-4410
(630) 961-3900
Fax: (630) 961-2168
www.sourcebooks.com

Printed and bound in China.
OGP 10 9 8 7 6 5 4 3 2

CONTENTS

MY
QUANTUM
LEAP

> *"It is not in the stars to hold our destiny but in ourselves."*
>
> —WILLIAM SHAKESPEARE

My personal ***quantum leap*** to where I am today as one of Mary Kay's top Independent National Sales Directors is the result of overcoming many obstacles, twists, and turns in my life. These obstacles helped me not only to see my goals, but also to make a ***quantum leap*** toward achieving them. Let me tell you more about my personal story.

Growing up in a healthy, loving, well-adjusted home was a huge blessing. I had **no** idea what a gift my parents gave me until I was grown and had conversations with many people who had not experienced the same positive upbringing.

This foundation of my happy childhood provided me with a platform of kindness, courage, and confidence that eventually led me to my current position of Mary Kay Independent Elite Executive National Sales Director, where I passionately teach other Independent Beauty Consultants about leadership and inspire them to achieve a lifestyle that works for them.

When I was growing up, I was diagnosed with dyslexia. At that time, educators did not know how to identify or support this reading disorder. I put in a lot of extra time studying, using late-night reviews and verbalizing my answers since reading and writing took me so much longer. But my parents were educators, so excellence in school was **required**...*no excuses and no options*.

I learned to compensate for my difficulties with reading and writing by relying on my voice, and I developed a way of speaking that is a unique mixture of inspiration and humor. I use that skill to impact others as a motivational speaker. It's my passion to teach others about how they can become successful.

I attended Howard University as an undergraduate and had a great experience. I discovered that I **love** to work. I challenged myself in school and worked hard at a grocery store, taking on all the overtime I could get my hands on. Even in school, I knew I wanted to be in sales. I wanted to be a leader…and I wanted to be VERY successful.

After college, I took a job as a manufacturing supervisor and hated it! But, it was at that job that I learned the two most important things about changing the course of my life—about making a ***quantum leap***.

First,

I learned that where you
end up is entirely up to you.

Second,

I learned that even though change
might be scary, it is definitely required.

If I did not want to be at a job I hated forever—and I did *not*—I had to change. I decided to go back to school for an advanced degree despite the challenges of having dyslexia. I also decided to attend the best business school in the world: Harvard University's School of Business. Yes, the Harvard Business School!

My start there was a bit rocky. I failed my first exam! It was a four-hour written exam, and it took me all four hours to turn in

two sentences. But, with courage, I let the faculty know of my handicap, and I pushed through. It took a lot of **very** hard work, but I also learned the importance of asking for and receiving assistance from others. I actually had people read my Harvard Business School textbooks to me out loud.

Graduating from Harvard gave me the confidence that comes from fighting for your dream. Armed with my new MBA, I took a sales position created especially for professionals with advanced degrees. It was not the usual career choice for a Harvard graduate, but I took the challenge…and excelled! The experience solidified my confidence and strengthened my belief that I am someone who can achieve goals, even against all odds.

While I was successful in my sales position, another obstacle surfaced when I was promoted to a management position. Moving from commission to straight salary created a ceiling on earnings. I knew in my heart that the sky could be the limit for me if I pursued an entrepreneurial career—another **quantum leap**.

One of my friends invited me to attend a Mary Kay appointment. Seeing other successful and positive women helped me make the decision to try my own Mary Kay business. However, I didn't get overwhelming support from everyone. In fact, when I told my mother about my decision to leave a secure corporate job to start my Mary Kay business, she was shocked. She wondered what in the world I was thinking and could not comprehend how someone who worked so hard to receive a graduate business degree from Harvard would want to sell lipstick! (But when you really look at the Mary Kay opportunity, it is about *building people*—the vehicle is cosmetics!)

My mother didn't see the potential of entrepreneurship the same way I did. But there were personal reasons prompting my decision to launch my own business as a Mary Kay Independent Beauty Consultant.

I was just coming out of a ten-year marriage filled with domestic violence. No one knew of the terrible secret I harbored. I was not strong enough to leave the marriage for myself, but I was strong enough to leave for my children. I knew I had to make a change. I knew I needed a positive environment that was filled with people who believed in me. I wanted something totally different from what I was accustomed to; I was seeking an adventure that I could become wildly excited and passionate about. I needed a fresh start. Once I gathered the strength to change the direction of my life, that strength was mine to use over and over.

With a difficult divorce in front of me and a huge desire to improve my family's lifestyle and increase my income, I decided to live my DREAM, one day at a time.

I'm proud to say I achieved my own ***quantum leap***—and then some. I've attained the highest position in the Mary Kay independent contractor sales force as an Inner Circle Independent National Sales Director and broke a company record by achieving Independent Elite Executive National Sales Director faster than anyone in the company's fifty-year U.S. history. My Mary Kay business was the forum I needed to climb the ladder of success with all the heart I will describe in this book. I'm still excited for where I am going. Forward *and* up!

As a leader of leaders in my Mary Kay business, I've learned that so many people have started at the same place I did. They also want to excel and are **willing** to do the work if only they just knew **what to do!** To create a ***quantum leap***, you still have to do the obvious: work hard, have ambition, face your fears, and be willing to risk failure. The ten steps I've captured in this book helped me reach success, and they can help you, too.

So, join me in taking your own **quantum leap** to make your dreams a reality.

Here's to seeing you *Soar!*

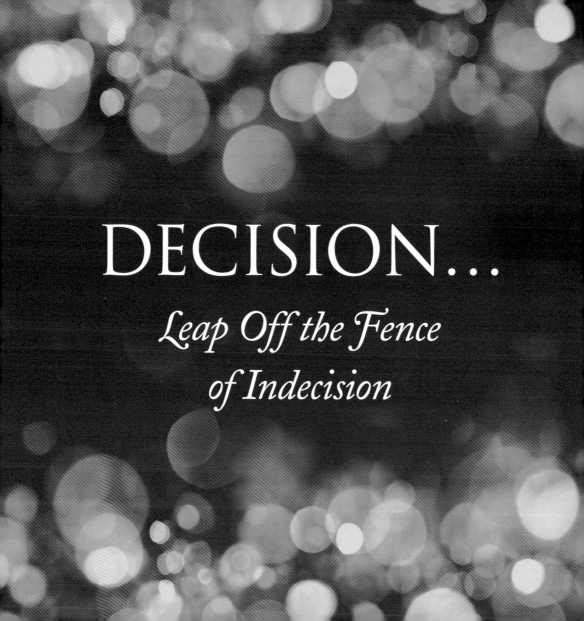

DECISION...
Leap Off the Fence of Indecision

"Go confidently in the direction of your dreams!
Live the life you've imagined."

—HENRY DAVID THOREAU

The first step to making a **quantum leap** is making a decision. You need to have a clear direction of where you are going. Many times, the freedom of having so many choices stops us from choosing **one**.

We often find ourselves on the fence of indecision, thinking, "What should I do? What do others think I should do?"

We start evaluating and judging our abilities, becoming discouraged about the possibilities before we even commit to a certain direction, goal, or outcome.

In my experience, a clear, specific definition of your intended direction is critical. If you do not know the destination, how will you know if you are off course?

There are many ways to reach a goal, but to experience a **_quantum leap_**, you have to reach your goal as quickly and efficiently as possible. You can't make that happen without clarity in your vision.

It was clarity of purpose that helped me break the first of many records in my Mary Kay business—but my path, as so many times before, was not a straight one.

I had attempted three times to build a team within a specific time frame. I wanted to meet this goal so badly because I knew this achievement would have a great impact on my lifestyle. So I went to work—reading and gathering ideas, listening to those who went before me, and trying various options.

The **result?** Failure, failure, failure. I became sick and tired of people telling me that failure was full of lessons. I had gotten that message a long time ago, and I did **not** need it again, thank you.

Then I did something masterful. I went to a retreat and placed myself in an environment that causes change. The speakers and stories made me feel as though it was "my time." I said to myself, "Enough is enough. I am tired of **my** attitude of 'I'll *try*.'"

I prevailed, I built my team, and I broke the record as well. Nothing had changed except the clarity of my vision. The company didn't change, the products didn't change, and my approach didn't change. What did change was my clarity about where I was going, what it would look like, and how I wanted to build it. I became committed to making the change happen **now.** With that decision, obstacles started to move out of my way. With faith and clarity, my path became crystal clear. In the next four months, I broke a huge twenty-six-year-old company record against tremendous odds.

To create a **quantum leap**, you have to **really** want it. I call it moving from the "Want To Lane" to the **"Got To Lane."** Is this just something you have been thinking about, talking about, or *complaining about*, or is this a clear decision that you are ready to **do something about**?

When you have chosen to
take action, you have crossed
into the *Decision Zone*.

MAKE A DECISION.

"The size of a person is determined by what it takes to stop him."

—Dr. Howard Hendricks

CONFIDENCE...

The Platform
for Charisma

> *"Believe in yourself! Have faith in your abilities! Without a humble but reasonable confidence in your own powers you cannot be successful or happy."*
>
> — NORMAN VINCENT PEALE

Without a doubt, *confidence* is necessary for a **quantum leap**. The most exciting thing about confidence is that it is dynamic and can be constantly strengthened as you reach new positions on your ladder of success.

People are drawn to confident people—those who look, act, and are sure of themselves. When I walk into an appointment, I put on my most confident look, I stretch out my right hand with an extended straight arm, I look the person right in the eye, and I add a **big** smile.

My body language says, "I'm fun, I'm feminine, I'm professional, and I'm here for business." Not one word has to be exchanged. My persona exudes **confidence.** Sometimes, though, you find yourself in situations where you have no idea what to do and you definitely don't feel confident. In that case, *you fake it until you make it.*

Parenting is a perfect example. Sometimes, you have no clue how to handle things. When you first bring your new baby home, you are very cautious about everything you do. But after you see that your best choices are smart enough to guide a **life**, you feel more confident in making the many decisions you need to make as a parent. Small successes build your confidence as the provider, the protector, the parent.

Confidence is a differentiator in every area of your life.

I wish I had a dollar for every time I've heard "I have never done anything like that before." Everyone who has ever changed jobs has done things they have never done before; all you need is the confidence that you have the ability to learn the job.

Think back to a previous challenge, when you thought you couldn't possibly overcome the obstacle in front of you. Did you rise to that challenge? Of course you did.

We all need to be brought back to a place where we remember how strong we really are, and then use that renewed confidence over and over.

When I first achieved the status of Inner Circle Independent National Sales Director, I felt I had to start all over again. Before I achieved this goal, I was at the top of the tier below this status, and then I was at the bottom of the best, the bottom of the highest status. So I took a deep breath and drew upon what worked for me in the past:

★ **SIT BACK AND OBSERVE.** Accept that you are there because you earned it and because you are **good.**

★ **IDENTIFY YOUR GIFTS.** You won't find them by comparing yourself to others. You'll find them by paying attention and believing what many others have told you.

★ **STEP OUT THERE.** Be yourself. You have always figured it out before. You will again this time. Just remember, mistakes are part of the process. There's no way around them.

Make a conscious decision to build confidence. Here are some tips:

Build on small successes

Confidence is developed over time. You can see the difference in your decisions and performance as your confidence grows. For example, the first time you are asked to do a presentation, you will feel nervous. Your mouth will be dry, you'll be sweating, and thoughts will be spinning in your head. But, do a presentation on Monday, another one on Wednesday, and then *another* one on Friday, and you'll soon feel more confident. You will actually be looking for someone to ask you to present. Small successes that happen close together are key to building confidence.

Study what you do not know

Knowledge is powerful. Just knowing the information, even if you **never** use it, helps to build confidence.

Let's say you know nothing about cars, and you have *no* money. If your car breaks down, I bet you will research the best way to repair it for little or no cost!

Once you understand what you are talking about, you can go to the garage better prepared to tell the mechanic, "I want this done to my car, and I will pay only this amount for the repair."

You walk away with a payment agreement and are standing straighter than before, even as you catch the bus home until your car is fixed.

Confidence is the platform for charisma. It is the support that gives you the courage to change. It allows you to acknowledge the wisdom you possess and the courage to share that wisdom with others. Confidence drives you to walk into a room where you don't know anyone. It makes your light shine so brightly that others will want to know **who you are**.

Confidence is the "it" factor for those who excel.

"*If we all did the things we are really capable of doing, we would literally astound ourselves.*"

—THOMAS EDISON

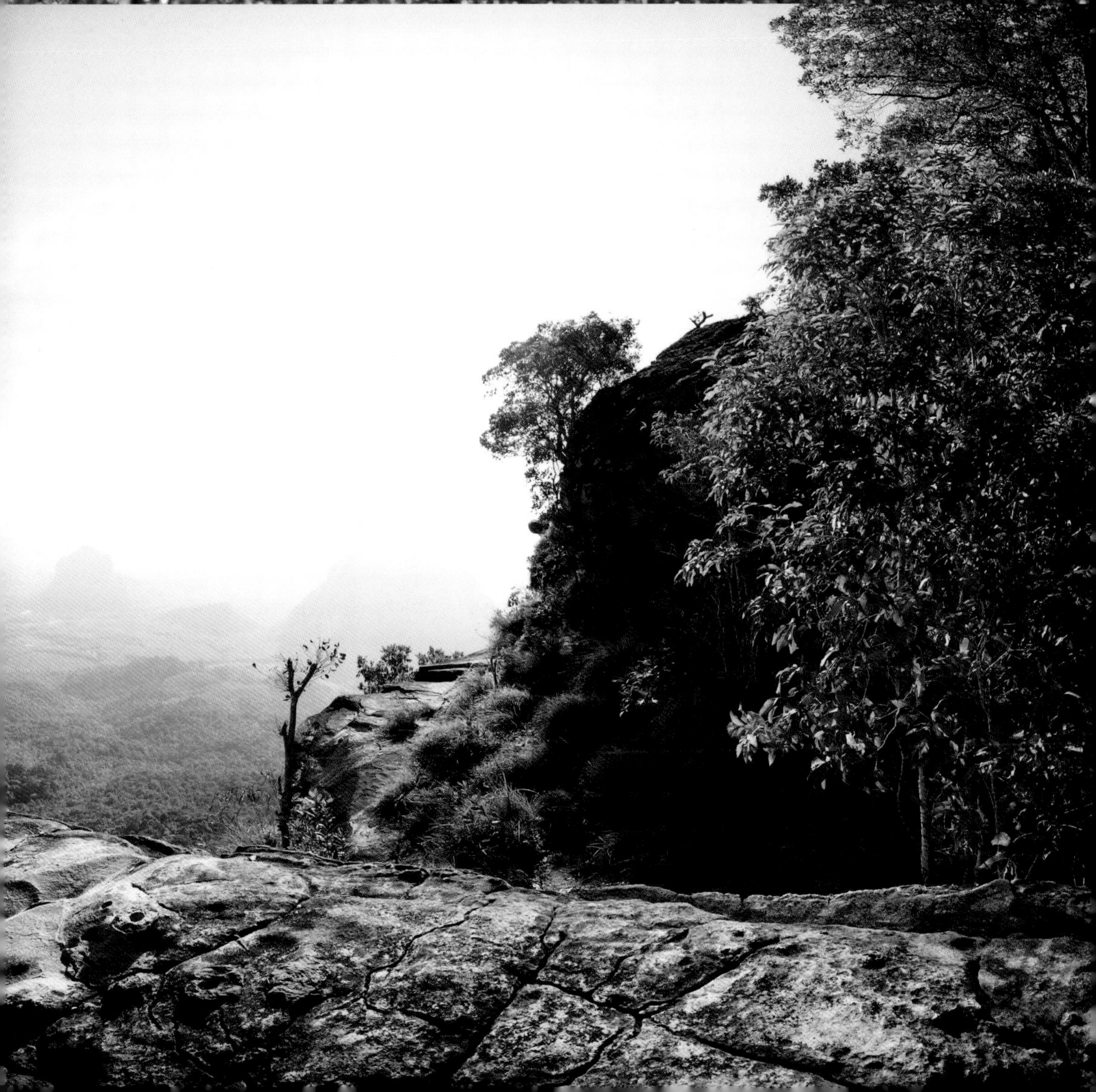

> *"To be a champ, you have to believe in yourself when no one else will."*
>
> —SUGAR RAY ROBINSON

Napoleon Hill said, "Whatever the mind of man can conceive and believe, it can achieve."

When you achieve your goal, you will have a **quantum leap**.

It all starts with a vision. If you want to end up in a different place, you have to see it first. When I first heard Napoleon Hill's words, I was very excited. Then I started wondering, "I can think it, but do I really believe it? I want to excel, I want to be a top performer and a leader who is acknowledged for my work, but do I **believe it**?"

I knew I needed to be able to develop my belief in my ability to achieve success in order to be able to teach others to do the same thing.

One step in building your belief is visualizing your success before it actually happens. Seeing it in your mind's eye helps you work toward the outcome. Visualization decreases doubt and prevents those negative thoughts that love to play in your head.

See yourself living in the neighborhood you imagine, in the corner office you desire, or in an outfit two sizes smaller. Tell the story the way you visualized it all along.

Your ability to see your success is imperative. Once you can see it, you can *own* it. Other people's doubts about what you are creating will not be able to penetrate your conviction or slow the actions you need to take to achieve your vision.

But how can you get to the point where you can see it? That's when you need to develop your "imagination muscle," the one that was super strong when you were a kid. Like all muscles, the "imagination muscle" loses strength if you don't use it.

When you were a child, you used your imagination and **believed** in whatever you were playing.

But then life started to happen: disappointments happened, friends let us down, boyfriends turned us away, we lost the job, or the contract on the home we really believed we were going to get fell through. Our imagination gets tired. We don't want to use it anymore. What for? Rejection after rejection. Rejection convinces us that we don't want to be disappointed ever again.

Before you realize it, you are stuck in the rut of life, going **nowhere** fast. You don't dream, you don't believe, and now your conversation is focused on what is wrong with the world instead of creating possibilities.

But once you exercise your "imagination muscle," you'll start to see the benefits. Here's an example:

Suppose you earn free plane tickets to the Caribbean island of your choice. You ask friends about the islands they love. You research different places, beaches, and activities. Your imagination kicks in because you **know** you are going—you already have the tickets. The possession of something tangible starts the process of dreaming, visualizing, and imagining. All of a sudden, all the commercials you see on TV feature palm trees and people who are relaxed. Everybody is wearing swimsuits.

Your imagination starts the Law of Attraction in motion, bringing forth what you visualize. The next thing you know, your dreams become reality.

First thing in the morning or over lunch, take a minute to have a positive conversation with positive people. Start using your imagination!

Vision, imagination, and *belief* make a **quantum leap**

POSSIBLE.

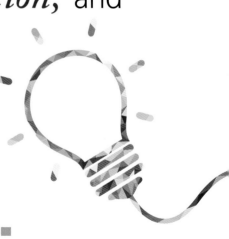

"*Vision is the art of seeing what is invisible to others.*"

—Jonathan Swift

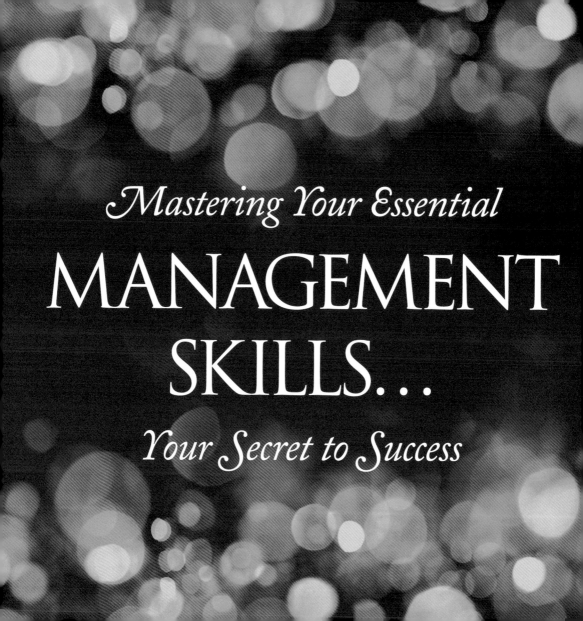

Mastering Your Essential

MANAGEMENT
SKILLS...

Your Secret to Success

> *"We must all suffer from one of two pains: the pain of discipline or the pain of regret. The difference is discipline weighs ounces while regret weighs tons."*
>
> —JIM ROHN

Managing your time, emotions, money, and skills can boost you up or keep you down. When you are ready to create a **quantum leap**, you must have these four areas under control. I always ask the question, "If you are not moving in the direction you want fast enough, what is slowing you down? Time, emotions, money, or skill management?" Usually, one of these is the main obstruction, but if managed successfully, you can quickly move toward your goals.

Time Management

For instance, you want to know my **best** time management tip? Put your keys in the exact same location all the time. How often do you look for your keys? Is there anything that makes you frustrated faster than looking for something you **just** had?

Simple decisions make the biggest difference. The power is in the details when it comes to managing your time.

Here are two other tips:

1. MAKE A LIST

Making a list is one of my favorite things to do. Honestly, sometimes I spend too much time making lists instead of working off the list. But, when you do a true brain dump, you will feel much better.

2. OVERCOME BEING OVERWHELMED

Taking big strides in the right direction when you are overwhelmed is **not** possible. It's similar to the feeling you get when you are driving to a new location.

You come to a three-way fork in the road. You have to make a decision **right now**. You feel overwhelmed. It is the exact same feeling you have when you see your desk and stuff is everywhere. Tons of emails are waiting for you **and** you keep having new ideas, but you haven't finished the **great** ideas you started last night.

But you have to move toward your destination. So you pick a direction and hope it's the right one. In thirty seconds, you will either say, "Wow, I'm good," or you will have to pull over, look at the GPS, call the appointment to tell them you'll be late, and turn around and drive in the right direction. Directions are just another list, you know.

Emotional Management

Emotional management partners with time management. Time management is making the list, but you also need to be prepared to leave in time to handle the unexpected.

When you are overwhelmed and emotions are invited to the party, you can feel the disappointment of a poor decision for *hours* and often indulge in negative self talk.

I should have used my GPS; everyone is going to look at me when I walk in late. Why do I do this every time?

You tell the story over and over again to whoever will hear it. But ask yourself, "Is what I am thinking or doing taking me in the direction of my dream?" If the answer is yes, you are headed to a **quantum leap**. If the answer is no, you are at a **roadblock** and you aren't going anywhere fast. You are moving slowly—or not at all.

My best emotional management tip is using the skill of *compartmentalization.* Everyone has emotions; they are part of our release mechanism. But, for many emotions, you can create a start and stop time. For example, when you are mad at someone, do you really **have** to be mad all day long? Does an argument have to hang on and on and on? Can you put yourself in check fast enough so you can be effective? If you are sad, and if you allow yourself to wallow in that sadness, you'll find yourself depressed and overwhelmed.

A good friend says the most expensive party you ever go to is a pity party.

There is a time and a place to display your emotions. Just be mindful and use your emotions to help you move in the direction of your dreams.

Money Management

Another key skill to master is money management. We all want to increase our incomes, and sometimes we **need** to increase our incomes.

To manage your money well, you have to make clear decisions about it. You need to have a budget (really hard for some); you must decide what you will invest and determine where you will sacrifice to move your agenda forward. You also need to determine whether your level of risk tolerance is a help or hindrance to making important financial decisions.

Money is one of those areas where I really believe expert help is required if you don't naturally have the "money management gene." It doesn't matter how many articles you read; you'll still struggle with your finances. If you work with people who have the gene, it's their passion. They have a knack for it; they read books and magazines about it because they *like to.* They can put together a plan for your money and help you to reduce your level of stress.

Skill Management

Skills give you the edge you need and are often the determining difference between success and failure. You can learn to master the skills you need from those who are more experienced. When you work hard at a skill, others will start calling it your talent. Some of the most talented and successful people master their skills through hard work, discipline, repetitiveness, experience, and just the determination to **get this**.

Your proficiency can give you the foundation and the confidence for the ***quantum leap*** you are ready to create.

"*Excellence is not a skill. It is an attitude.*"

—Ralph Marston

GOALS...

Make Them S-M-A-R-T

> *"Our goals can only be reached through a vehicle of a plan, in which we must fervently believe, and upon which we must vigorously act. There is no other route to success."*
>
> — PABLO PICASSO

Goals are the favorite word of ambitious people. Just give me a target to hit, and watch me focus on it. If I do not hit it the first time, I will be relentless until I do.

To have a **quantum leap**, there are important goal-setting tools and strategies that make a difference.

S-M-A-R-T Goals

Run this test *every* time you set a goal. Ask yourself if your goal is:

S—Specific

M—Measurable

A—Attainable

R—Realistic

T—Time-bound

Once you have a specific, measurable goal, you can create very important benchmarks. Benchmarks prove progress. Progress builds confidence.

"What you get by achieving your goals is not as important as what you become by achieving your goals."

—HENRY DAVID THOREAU

IMAGE...

Connect with Those Around You

> *"The person we believe ourselves to be will always act in a manner consistent with our self-image."*
>
> —BRIAN TRACY

Seven seconds. That's how long it takes to make an impression when a person first sees you. Better make it count.

Making a connection with people is key. Make it a good impression with your outfit, posture, handshake, voice level, hairstyle, and smile. Do you look like you care about yourself and those around you? Your look makes a statement!

Often, the cars we drive create the buzz we are looking for. Yet, there are many people who don't care about what they drive or wear. It's the way they treat people that leaves them pondering, "How did he make me feel **so** great in just that short period of time? How in the world did he remember my name?"

Image has a tremendous impact on how you make a person feel. Dr. Maya Angelou said, "I've learned that people will forget what you said, people will forget what you did, but people will never forget how you made them feel."

Your image can also have a tremendous effect on how **you** feel. When you think you look amazing, your energy is increased and you walk with pep in your step. You feel happier when you have taken the time to bring out your best. That feeling turns quickly into confidence and positive energy that draws people to you.

When you walk into the room, light up the place. Make the first person you see feel amazing. When you focus on your image and on other people, they will want to work with you, to serve you, and to be served by you.

"*Behavior is the mirror in which everyone shows their image.*"

—Johann Wolfgang von Goethe

> *"Passion is energy. Feel the power that comes from focusing on what excites you."*
>
> — OPRAH WINFREY

Can there be a **quantum leap** without passion? Is that possible? I have seen some great things happen, but a **quantum leap** without passion is **not** one of them.

Even when you are doing what you love to do, sometimes you operate with passion and sometimes without.

Without passion, you go through your day doing just what needs to get done, but there is no creative energy, no new ideas, no new joy. Life is just okay. The next thing you know, one day has passed, then a month, then a year…

Passion changes everything. When you work with passion, it is so much more powerful and impactful. A challenge, a deadline, or an event can cause passion to appear. There is now something that requires more of you and that helps you to embrace the outcome. You understand the benefits and rewards and become significantly interested in the success of the job at hand.

Passion makes a difference in every area of your life. You realize how much you have missed it. You love the way life unfolds when you are passionate about your efforts. You are joyful about who you are, and your energy level increases so much that you hate to go to bed because your mind is continually racing with **great** ideas.

You start thinking big, really **big**. You are clear, ready, willing, and **excited**. Your confidence grows when you become passionate. Nobody can stop you or even tries to get in your way.

When you operate with passion, solutions to problems or challenges present themselves and doubt disappears. "Failure is **not** an option" is written all over you.

When you want to make a **quantum leap**, it's important to understand what drives your personal passion. It is different for each person, and it is driven by what you value, how it affects those you love, its relevance to your career, or just how it makes you feel. My passion comes from the race; I love a deadline, I revel in breaking records, and I enjoy the competition. My passion brings out the best in me. What does it do for you?

Passion can shift your perspective from fear of failure to one of embracing success. It changes your thoughts and, therefore, your behavior and your results.

Know what creates *passion* for you and *reignite it* often.

"Every great dream begins with a dreamer. Always remember, you have within you the strength, the patience, and the passion to reach for the stars to change the world."

—HARRIET TUBMAN

DISCIPLINE
AND HUSTLE...
Make Things Happen

"Discipline is the bridge between goals and accomplishment."

—JIM ROHN

It's easy to do what you *want* to do. Everyone has that down pat. But you can't have a **quantum leap** without discipline—doing what you need to do even when you do not feel like it.

Discipline does not always show up just because you made a decision to do something. You learn discipline by continually exercising your "discipline muscles." Here are some things to keep in mind:

1. Start with small steps. Instead of saying, "I'll **NEVER** eat candy again," say, "I will never buy candy at gas stations anymore" (if that is your regular stomping ground for getting your sugar fix). **START SMALL.**

2. Find a result you **REALLY** want and that requires discipline. Choose a result you will experience quickly to increase your belief that you can do it. Once, when I was working to meet a quarterly sales goal, I knew I had one month left to achieve this goal. Suddenly, I was excited to work late, come in early, even work through lunch. Distractions did not stop me. I picked up the phone and started

making just one call—over and over. Did I win? You bet I did. Did I love the sensation? You bet!

3. Instead of focusing on discipline, focus on the **DESIRE.** When your desire is strong, it can help you quickly make decisions that were once hard. For instance, if your friend calls you and asks you to be in their wedding, you might realize that everyone will be looking at you while you are walking down the aisle. Up until this moment, you have **LOVED** dessert. You choose restaurants because of the dessert menu. But right after this phone call, cake starts looking awful to you. The desire to look your best makes your "discipline

muscles" stronger so that skipping your satisfying "sweet tooth" to be your best later becomes much easier. A sign on my bathroom mirror reads, "Don't give in to what you want now for what you want most." I look at it every day.

4. Acknowledge when you are procrastinating. We spend a lot of time convincing ourselves that what we are choosing to do in the moment is more important than what we **SHOULD** be doing.

Focus requires discipline, and there are many distractions. Email, Facebook, Twitter, TV. Realize that distractions are **everywhere**.

Hustle is being willing, capable, and available to do whatever it takes to get through it, around it, over it; whatever it takes to get the job done. Hustle shows up when failure is **not** an option. Passion is the push behind the hustle, but doing whatever must be done is the key.

Go after your dream with all your might. Working works when thinking won't.

"Good things happen to those who hustle."

—ANAÏS NIN

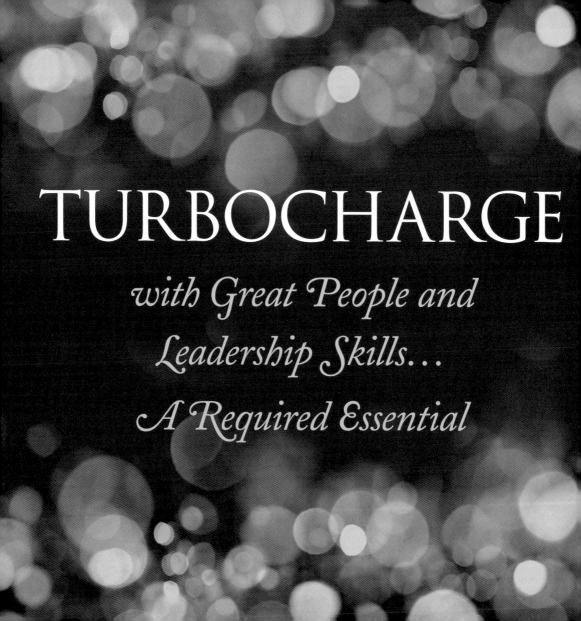

TURBOCHARGE

with Great People and
Leadership Skills…

A Required Essential

> *"The most important single ingredient in the formula of success is knowing how to get along with people."*
>
> —THEODORE ROOSEVELT

Creating a **quantum leap** in your life without strong people skills makes the road longer and **harder**.

Your goal should be to make everyone you come into contact with feel better.

Here are some of the benefits of increasing your people skills:

1. People will like you.

2. You will be more comfortable and confident.

3. You will make people feel better when they are with you.

4. You will feel more secure.

5. Your ability to build team spirit will be powerful, and your team leadership will be effective and enjoyable.

6. Focusing your attention on improving your people skills can improve both your own attitude and that of others.

7. You'll bring out the **BEST** in others, making your influence dynamic. When you help others deliver their best efforts, you'll work in turbo power because things will get **DONE.**

8. Improving your people skills helps reduce stress. Think about it—when you are happy and secure, you operate at your best and stress is reduced.

No matter how advanced our technology, it is still people who are the driving force of getting things accomplished. Improve your people skills, and you'll make great strides in positioning yourself for a **quantum leap**.

"Pretend that every single person you meet has a sign around his or her neck that says, **'MAKE ME FEEL IMPORTANT.'** *Not only will you succeed in sales, you will succeed in life."*

—MARY KAY ASH

SHORT-TERM SACRIFICE...

Take the Long View,
It's Worth It

"Self-development is a higher duty than self-sacrifice."

—Elizabeth Cady Stanton

Give up your distractions until the job is done.

Even though you may want to accomplish something that means a lot to you, distractions can hold you back from your key priorities.

Sometimes you have to make a decision to change things for a moment, to stop doing what you want to do in order to start having what you want to have. Make a short-term sacrifice and watch the **MAGIC** happen.

I've seen this work again and again in my own life. For example, I **love** the movies, the feeling of melting away in a world that does not exist for a few hours. It's a pleasure I shared with my friends every week.

But when I was developing my leadership skills, I needed to use every valuable moment to focus and finish what I set out to do. There were a lot of movies I did not see, even though I wanted to see them.

My short-term self-sacrifice paid off...and then some.

Once you make the decision and start acting on it, you may start seeing positive results and the sacrifice becomes easier.

When the goal seems far away, cut the job down to size by dividing it into smaller components. We are more capable of landing on the mark when it is in sight. Making short-term sacrifices and meeting short-term goals help build confidence.

Your Goal—

and your ***quantum leap*—*

are within

YOUR REACH.

CONCLUSION

Choose to shake up the world.

Decide to take it by storm. Take **big** juicy
steps up the ladder of success.

Break records; let others see you take the lead
with **passion** and joy.

Take others with you along the way, and be the
example that others can follow.

Create a song others enjoy playing because it
makes them better people.

Life is short; take *quantum leaps* to the top.

See the view from the top, get comfortable,
and become **confident.**

Use your gifts and leave your stamp on the
world through your *quantum leap*!

ABOUT THE
Author

Dr. Gloria Mayfield Banks, described by many as "energy in motion," is a woman of many accomplishments. She has a Harvard MBA and an honorary doctorate from the University of Maryland–Eastern Shore and is a renowned motivational success strategist, a multimillionaire entrepreneur, and a Mary Kay Independent Elite Executive National Sales Director. Growing up in a loving family in Detroit, Michigan, Gloria was the third of four girls born to parents who were both educators. At an early age, Gloria's parents discovered she struggled with reading, which was later diagnosed as dyslexia. Despite the challenge, Gloria never considered dyslexia a handicap, just another obstacle to overcome. Gloria graduated from Howard University and began her career as a sales representative for IBM. She later joined Stratus Technologies as a manufacturing marketing manager and went on to become assistant director of admissions at the Harvard University School of Business, where she traveled nationally and internationally to recruit students. Gloria has since counseled and encouraged victims of domestic violence and lobbied in Washington, DC, as an advocate for domestic violence prevention.

Faced with being a single mother and dealing with a difficult divorce, Gloria began her Mary Kay business to supplement her income. Within eighteen months, she set new company sales

3

ing3

records and later grew her business to more than $24 million in area retail sales and an area of more than six thousand Independent Beauty Consultants. Her record-breaking ascent to Independent Elite Executive National Sales Director was faster than anyone in the company's fifty-year U.S. history. Gloria is one of only three women in the United States to become a Mary Kay Independent Elite Executive National Sales Director. Today, she has expanded her entrepreneurial influence to include not only her record-breaking Mary Kay business, but also her co-ownership of a marketing, product, and promotional events company. She is happily married to her husband, Ken, and they share four adult children and three grandchildren and reside in Baltimore, Maryland.